Escape This Crazy Life of Tears

(JAPAN, JULY 2010)

NORMAN FISCHER

Escape This Crazy Life of Tears
(JAPAN, JULY 2010)

NORMAN FISCHER

TINFISH

Tinfish Press is a 501(c)3 non-profit, tax-exempt corporation
that supports the publication of experimental poetry from the
Pacific. Tinfish books are available from Small Press Distribution
in Berkeley, California, (spdbooks.org) and from our website.

Susan M. Schultz, Editor

47-728 Hui Kelu Street #9
Kāneʻohe, HI 96744
www.tinfishpress.com

Thank you to the Left Wing Right Brain Fund of the Hawaiʻi
Community Foundation and to other donors for their kind con-
tributions toward the publication of this book.

ISBN-13: 978-0-9891861-3-1

Designed by Allison Hanabusa

To all the dedicated practitioners of Everyday Zen, those who accompanied me on this pilgrimage, and the many others. With gratitude for your love, energy, and devotion.

JULY 10. 10. KYOTO

It's icelush

Swirkle

While not regarding

The street – swell

And not as hot

As advertised

Her vision without compromise

Noteworthy and bad

Handwriting

In Germany

Local color

This is not   Germany

.

Two girls sitting at table

Talking, hand gestures,

Drinking coffee – and us here

Kohee.   **Kohee.**

It's cookie chow!!

.

Music, crowds

At Pure Water Temple

Abuts forest

Green   Tea   Ice

.

JULY 11. 10. KYOTO

Pure Water Temple

Home of kami, old, very old

You can't argue with that

.

"May we be your guide?

We are University girls

Practice English"

.

Rings hand-bell,

Alms to priest

Bowing, blessings, word-tones

Big straw hat leggings   :

Martha's pal!

Water – for love

Beauty, long life

or

Wisdom

I choose

Beauty

since

You can have only one

Kenninji Temple

Dogen's old home

Wind god dance

Thunder god dance – very

Famous

Video of talking

Priest, square frame

Floats in dark

.

16 Arhats

Photo I took

Before because

The same things

Keep on impressing me

.

Lost my hat

At restaurant

No, it is

On my head

.

Looking all over

For hat it is

On my head

.

Hat on head

Weather hot, it is

Nearly my hat

On my head

.

Pure Water Temple

Kodanshi

Muromachi

Or some style,

Some period

.

Nenni founded it

Widow of Shogun

Ordained when he died

.

Pair of

Sen-no-rikkyu teahouses

Joined by walkway

One has two stories,

No other two story

Teahouse in all Japan

Old very old, no arguing

With that

.

Wearing neat samue

Men and women in uniform

All neat, uniform

Oh let's buy good mokugyo!

.

Uh oh, lost mokugyo

And my hat, hat is

On my head

.

OK, Peter has got mokugyo

Brown paper bag

Good sound, for home

.

Walkway, walkway, walkway

Gravel gardens, sans plants

OK maybe one pine tree

Propped up by bamboo

SONY

Icelush! Icelush!

Nature donut!

Summer chance.

Summer choice.

.

Light and easy

Kohee, sugar toast

.

Milling crowd

Shellacked mackerel

Tasty

.

Milling crowd

Rain possibly

Noodle vending machine

.

Coffee vending machine

Oh green tea !

Sound of many voices murmur

Many words are none, humming

      soft rumble

.

Many voices

Speak at once

Not human sound

         -    **illumined grasses**

   waiting to be seen

On the train

Moving trees and houses

Wavering wordlets

.

Things rise,

Fall,

Melt away

Having lost

      the

      mokugyo,

The

      hat, found

      the

Camera,

      the

      cat

.

Row of rings

White rings,

White love

.

Buddhas from the moist earth

Darkly emerge

Beneath bamboo

.

Rain, then

    more rain

Buddhas, then

    more Buddhas

.

Sliding paper windows

A conception of heaven –

Penetrating light-beams over sea

.

Conception of hell – fire

Poured down throat

Pliers twist tongue

Twin mountains crush tiny

Frightened

    naked

    people

Rushing through

Bird-beaked demons

Fiery-headed – ring-staffed

Jizo protects

Children whom

demons

torture

With task-frustrations

Endless fire, endless rain

Can't read the signs

Don't know

        the words

    illumined grasses, tint

  time

Ruth's camera records

what was but a word's word's

undepicted, neither its

sound, face, nor

    meaning

reverberates, shutters, a time being

tincture...   **tint...**

All wear samue, rakesu

This religion: "pray I pass

My exam. A thousand

      Cranes"

Tiles, a man plasters

Such smooth

Moves, cloth

Wrapped round forehead, duck

Feet

.

Gate, gate — wall, wall,

--- on through,   up

against

.

seaweed, fish-paste

foreign to

a foreigner

.

up into mountain,   a fox

mountain potato,   sweetened

close quarters, wall ;   gate

.

rain, pelts, slants or

not, waits in

car port -----   cemetery, **illumin-**

      ated grass, it's go in

        that ----- or now, ----- mark-

           ed up,   heat is down

      Zen wood

.

Temple burned down, all walls,

Gates re-built in rain

Profusion of plants, as tropical

Re-made ----- re-done, as

      before   **not just**

        this **,**   **carrying**

The entire past, clap twice, ring

      bell – sometimes good

Sometimes bad – sneaky fox,

The Lord giveth the Lord taketh away

bird-beaked demons

in both cases,   on either   side

built shaky bridges   into   the

                    Pure   Land

                    .

Easy to do, harder not to

                            do,   ,   crisp ,

as fish when dead, shape

contoured   for   speed

                    .

that shape, the whole past is

                    now,   too

just that fast, the Lord taketh

Based on partial knowledge

                    .

A piece,   page

Very good in that regard

I said some things

                                        hard   to   tell

--------- **attack!**

             tatari.   ta   ta   ri.

open to question.   but not

             my family, your family

             why my mother   wasted

             away, she becomes incontinent

loses her appetite, always falls

                      down

             "causes and conditions are vast"

             this is the life

             there is enough money

or not

             it's your fault, mine

             so much more to it

                      than

                                        that

             .... and less than

                      that's

""""""""""""""all the more so

             .

vermillion gates up   into

       the   forest   fox

her words - *her* force

absence makes more power

because there's nothing

now

        but -----

                 that,

water, water, falls from sky

quartz, crystal

          pure —

      a wish , it

   simply falls , falls

   this way , earth-

      ward

wanted , feeling   adhered to

     ,

    a cry , a crowd,

  each one   sufficient

   to speak slow or

         quick

some explanation necessary

      for what happens

to be free of blame

 .

these stones, such

up   and   down,

scooped , horizontal   weighty as dead

        beached whale

vertical , huddled , bent

     as

     Rodin's Balzac

   as dark, a harmony, in

relation   in   raked

    sand

      ..... and then

           moss

       mounds, 5

      to one

         side

   green in pelting rain

shards , sheets   of rain

    as flattened rags

hurled off roof-edge

        dissolve in air

        flooding gravel

       air's moist abundance

..... quickly moving clouds

  .

who   has   such   sense

of   beauty   exquisite   quiet

sensa   bility   who   has

such   quiet   feeling   now

    rain   stops,   air's

  gray,   quiet   -----   trees

                trees

                trees

        green   pine   trees

  .

lotusleafcup   holds

    waterdrop   bundle

rolling

silver

gem

.

Can't   be   social

any   more

approximate

person   ,   exhausted

But couldn't be so

       in another   place

          always it's

go   **in**

this   one

sigh , big bold red

        Chinese roof ,

   National Treasure

.

Gates, corporate sponsored

    foxes , too

        clap twice

        ring bell

pray for good things

.

frozen snow in horizontal

sheets   much   wished

for

this hot summer day

.

At first rain was

feared

then   we   saw

yes   rain's   immense

time's   such   perfection

.

going , then gone

.

Hojo's four gardens

Stones, mosses, five hills,

Squares, irregular

Mounds, shapes, a

rim , dividing

and

divided

heaven   ,   earth

order

all's in place

fading.......

.

dozo

o-hiyo

gozaimasu

itadaki

masu

peanuts   ,   crackers

bubble tea

.

Kawaramachidori, Tera-

machi   dori

watch out for

"THE CRAB"

.

The past : you can't

    argue

        with that

.

sea with no exit

.

spewing rain

splatters on streets

shattering drops

burst with light, silver

carhisssss   ,   umbrellas

    float   by

.

Spain wins World

    Cup   , later

Japanese piano man plays

    Billy Strayhorn tune

JULY 13.10. KYOTO.

Lazy day , last

name of Buddha

as "fool"

Eel   -   all sorts

pickle

pop   off   personality

whole   squid , pink

small fish heads

umeboshi   plum

eat one a day

for longevity

.

it's not in the   way

things   are   done

not

in the sun-face   - to see

as, how

things are,

are done

not the smiling face

painful to be

ashamed   -   have

not

done

enough

for the other:

never have

:

thick   green   bamboo

and   new

bamboo   violates

its   wasted   sheath

it's not in knowledge

or simple

country knowing

not in details —

"streets have no names!

houses have no numbers!" —

that we can

see

.

small cars , narrow

streets

careful   driving

.

Myoshinji precincts

old stone paved

path , small

temples - trees,

bush,

flowers

you wind back down

     there

    see guardian lion

      on roof

  .

sake, peanuts, pickles

    crumpled okesa

      on table , being

        repaired , too

    much worn long

     ago

  .

the past: not to be

    denied

  .

old priest walks by

light green rakusu, white

zori, black robe, slightly

bent as he goes – down Myoshinji

lane, not in a hurry . Woman

coming out new temple door

with neat black plastic bags of

garbage gets in tiny red car

drives away without a glance,

invisible　.　School kids in

black and white uniforms

led by guide in black and white

giggling, talking, being

respectful　. Young priest in

room near Hojo , somber in

robes, sitting formal, studies

text, facing open door

"Konnichiwa."　Quiet,

quiet, old painted

screens　.

.

it's not　　　as

　　　　　surface　,　it's

　interpretive

depth　　　　makes　a

hierarchy　,　shame

you live   *under*   it

it comforts   ,   oppresses,

   if you're in it

      if you're out

.

a great human

      family , father , mother

         sons , daughters

.

   fire puja   , why not

protect the emperor, the

nation

each day

      just in

      case

.

surface   , exact   it's

      not that

you can't argue with that

it's *in* freezing snow-shrouded

   mist-shrouded mountain

         tree-tops, cryptomeria –

    cryptic   but

not in the names ,

    my being one isn't

            that – sorry

isn't it..........

   .

Dogen's ordination platform

    dark , mysterious ,   inside

    graffiti ; close in , but

      , *a flash* ,

    reveals interior

space too small for 1,000

monks – on Hiei, Enryakuji

Saicho ordained small

monks without all the

„ rules „

chant   sutra   here

see   trees

imagine feeling the past

-          you can't argue with

that

„„„„„„„„„„„„„„„„„" this   ....

(however imagined)

elegant meal for priests

ground   roots , mango ,

melon   , sweet

   mustard   , food

as eaten in the

         past..... then .....

as now ..... but now.....

as refracted by then is now

         as historical

now as then or

                         now

.

         bell

     reverberates

as that , sound

of past but

not as past as

imagined is now

as we are

so were not

.

sparrow , quail , roasted

    spread out on spit

    pure   poor

    glazed with sauce

.

green tea

bean paste

                sweet

.

Enryakuji made

Against Nara

Buddha too big ,

      Much intrigue

Can't beat 'em so

Establish capital elsewhere

Another temple , new

    Religion

.

portrait statue of Dogen   ,

    dark   soft   wood

        no

                          photosplease

  .

Dengyo Daishi's

    Standing Shaka

        Incense , bows

Trees drip with rain   ,

                    Haze ,

                    Mist

Lanterns line mountain

Running monks run

Ancient way   ,   to - day

  .

          the context

          behind what we

        do   ,   ancient

way

not any

context con-

text to this

immediate ex.............................

.

. .

high on mountain

bad spirits from the

northwest

protection　　　　　magik chanting

Dengyo Daishi's power

Awesome .... rain

Context

do - the

hall　, **it's go in**

illumined grass

so much *not* the case

.

floating mist   across

          parking lot - gray

                              gray

                         a way

protection from the

               northwest - bad

influences   from   there -

          be

                    ware

                    organs

                    made of cells

.

elaborate traditions

the stars   ,   the moon   ,   some

seasons   for   some

               flowers

          (campanula)

     tea   and   manju

        500 yen - now

                    but then

only a gift

gifts

on   in-

justice , the

only always

human

squeeze

.

injustice , heart of

hearts – words

haze   and   breeze

the   women   always

dying , they accept

that

then

not

break   suff

ring world

a-tilt

.

two nuns emerge from

car – Christian, Buddhist

                    ?

.

                    cryptomeria   ,   mist

bamboo bent with rain

        delicate   curved

                floating foliage   :

        silence   of   the

                teaching

.

they wear same headgear

of meditating Tendai monks

maybe 800, 900, then

cover the head in white

purify thought

raze   desire

.

I'd had a thought

Then – now – gone

Can't think of it

That thought yet thought's

Shape – and – memory

Linger still in me   , im-

Pressions of that which

      Had occurred

   In thought?

    In

      Fact? Is thought

      As thought

         Fact?

Fact of the matter

  .

      those curved roofs

thought's result – that

  shrouded statue and feeling

thought's result   , first thought

  then deed   and

  artifact   ,   past   , time-

  less   *(you can't*

can't   argue   with

    that/this)

then thought remembered

thought forgotten   ,   thought

 frozen in wood   ,   stone   ,

    paint – trace of person

(they undergo austerities,

    stay pure, vow not to

    leave mountain 12

years   ,   hear

        their voices

                in-

                        side

  .

raked pathways, curved

        lines

some thinking, thinking

        what

            ?

don't go   there

silent   respect

    do   not

enter   do

              not

              leave

.

path down   ,   steep stone

              steps

I recall monastery stones

no   stories   no   one's

              thought

              illumined

        just   that   light

              protects the nation

you   believe   that

so   it   is   so

              still   :   killing

              injustice

seems no tomorrow

              there

blood's bright

moisture

shining

.

JULY 14. 10. KYOTO

Gion Matsuri's start

    floats out on Shijo

       crowds of people

no cars

    tonight

.

at Matsumotoya

seated around table

in room   crowded

with boxes   no English

        and

    no   Japanese

.

hossu   , rakesu   , kogo ·

bessu   , jubon   , shuso

fans, half a dozen,

"Sendo - please

send to me — paying now,

arigato

.   .

Takashimaya's basement

food confusion : think,

        food

pickles   , Italian bread

with figs   , okashi   , lox

please   , thank you

.

zenga, scrolls, lovely

scrolls, artist's name,

Nantembo and his followers,

abbots here and there

takuhatsu monks all in crooked row

"of all the ways to practice

depending on others

is best" - all the

villages come out to help

robe hiked up, big round hat,

black robes like crows –

gift for you, our teacher,

heart's flow _____

three trips to sewing store

sewing boards, small,

medium, large , _____

,   ,

"these are very heavy

to carry round Japan"

Teamen since 1803

"Japanese way"   best tea

only cover   ,   hot water

leaves not open   ,   pour   ,   sip

tea not with meal   , to drink

but to sip   , twice   , three

times. , cover   , pour and sip

.

best tea picked in May

then   :   jar, pressed down hard

some air — hot vacuum —

then in Fall, leaves are brown

mix and blend

                                    but

some modern style say fresh

          is best

do not like to see brown leaves

foolish way of now — I

do not like to say so

I do not say so

many people   ,   many ways

.

husband, wife, scrolls, baskets

wife, husband, tea

.

inkens, please — sifters

for the chidens

summer jubans

.

behind all this — in-

      side

      isn't

the surface is that

hard and soft

interpretations, desires

sprayed-on meanings, reasons

to hold or avoid, to run

from, toward, source of pride

or dejection — is hot, cold,

hard, soft, learned meanings

the past is now

.

tall floats remembered

costumes , music , bells &

       drums

Genji's white-faced chigo

tippy & tall

.

To avert a pestilence

Caused by curse of Gozu Tenno

66 pillars erected at Shinsenen Garden

Gion gods propitiated, now

Each year as if then though

No pestilence these floats

Roll on as does pestilence

People die all the time, an epidemic,

Daily they do, so many

So many I had not thought

Death had undone so many

Nasty brown river rolls on

Wherever you go

Churning power overreaching

Its bounds

.

pickle party! pickle party!

sake,Asahi,cucumber

tiny fishes,chestnuts,rice

crackers,natto miso

still tinier fishes,eel,salmon

pickles! pickles! pickles!

etc.   etc.   etc.

eating,drinking,scrolls

hanging,Bodhidharma

&the begging monks

cheerful faces everywhere _____

.

JULY 15.10. YAMASHIRO

let   the   past

          be   past

let   the   present

          reflect   the   past

as   it   will   and

          must

let   not   the   past

          oppress   the   present

nor   the   present

          deny   the   past

.

green rice fields

      below green mountain

          covered in cloud & mist

water rushes by in streams

      over   rocks

      life   lived

      this   way

      as it   is

         here ,

      as in immediate surround

      you can't argue with

         that

.

an American foot

how can you measure

this   talk

in Greek   feet

Silk Road, East meets West

no East, no West

How we do it in our place

the way it's been done, as seen

as ordained — yes, it's

only that — the line's

neither long nor short

.

Hokkyoji   steep   stone

            path to gate

past gate to Hondo,

                    shokan

sampai   ,   raihai

Tanaka, Hojo-san, talks, relaxed

"A bully bullied one who

is subject to bullying , —

pressed heavy weight on

weak knees on

concrete — here he made

raihai — *SANZEN* raihai

3,000 bows

& carried the man round the Hondo

doing penance. Another man

cheated on his wife, did

            raihai, cleared

his soul — my gift to you:

            do

            raihai

            also   do

          at   least

three minutes of zazen a day

I don't say 'only' I say

            'at least'

which I do do, each

day, 47 years, 55th

abbot of Hokkyoji"

.

Translated by young

half-white boy, ordained a month ago

unsure of the sense

of what Hojo-san says

what does he mean

which is which (bully or

bullied), drenched in

painful self-consciousness

and awkward stage-fright

when Ruth, Kate, Michael or the

ex-soldier could have

easily done as well

with less mortification :

but it's him

Jumen (Chinese) met

Dogen at Tientong,

Tendo's place, seven

years his junior im-

pressed with serious Jap-

anese monk he came to

the wild country of kami

sat on mountain rock 18 years

as Mongols marched

the mountain pass

came down to found Hok-

yoji, then Gien planted

same cypress here he then

planted at Eiheiji, now 700

years gone by

.

big wooden fish

outside sodo, three

generations planned

"crack crack crack"

fish eyes don't ever close

always awake

      like sodo monks

"in many lives

we have practiced

together, all become

Buddha later on"

  .

side step up

down, Kai-

sando, incense

for Junnen, Gien

"thank you Mr.

Junen, Gien this

sincere practice"

  .

"First I thought

      teacher just like

Buddha then rebelled

ten, fifteen years

then very sick

ate barley only

very expensive

money gone

then Eiheiji raihai:

'please Mr. Dogen spare

this life I'll be good'

and did - & was –

47 years till now,

trying"

.

"so do what Mr.

Norman Feeshure tells

practice hard

in many lifetime

or a few

you also be

Buddha, honor

the past"

winter in Hokkyoji:

much snow piled

up on old roof

monks must knock

it down, dangerous

I will send

this snow

to America

if possible

small rain then

pelting rain, strong

rain's sound

pit pit drum,

hits earth

peaceful sound, rain

these green mountains

strong clear streams

sluice-way zigzag

down

mountainside, water

strong on rock, white

water's sound, religion

just a word, human

style – that sound

the many sounds of rain

truth's style, earth was

made to say – cloud says,

ear, heart, say

.

distant, lonely

sound   heard   only

by   me

.

Dogen's portrait

Only one painted

In his lifetime seen

On covers of all

The books in English

Puckered plum-blossom

Lips, thick square face,

Jutting jaw, distant eyes

Here! In Hokkyoji

Treasure House! – with

Dogen's own

Chinese poem

Ink still black

After 800 years

.

portrait of Tendo too

avuncular & kind:

"practice hard

not to get it

right – but it's

the only way

escape this

crazy life of tears"

.

Ungo Doyo's face

old picture of Mr Shakka

brought here by Junen

Junnen's wooden traveling

sutra box behind glass

reflecting own face, thank

you very much, photos,

gifts, good-bye

.

Why do they freeze

In unheated Hokkyoji

Why practice in those

Harsh conditions?

Old-time people believed

OK to die

In dharma pursuit

Good karma, better

Luck next time, otherwise

Despair, dejection, terror

And fear: no use

This worldly life

Anymore – go to Buddha's

Land, seek

Fòrtune – do

      Or

      Die

  .

different   , they're

just   like

      us

then   just like

      now

culture's meanings

all re-arranged, person's

not what she used to be

still –

      Uncle Death

conditions

         thought

big nothing blank indefinite

shapes   thought/feeling

so human's same

as ever – as quiet

—   as incomprehensible

as darkly different

In onsen, not the

onsen we expected

with streams & mountain

paths but *this* onsen in

a little ordinary town

all in neat yutakas,

red for women, blue for men

and salarymen in tubs

joking over jobs, old couples,

young couples with their broods

and we eating at fancy

buffet, sushi, tea, fancy rice

worldly things have

no meaning they are

the meaning, that they

are at all, not what's

assigned them by desire.

the past creeps up on them

covers them with its design

brings feeling to the heart.

in Eiheiji Hatto's perfect

movement thought of torah

scroll's procession through

shuel of my ancestors, kissing

it, the book: a book! no distant

shrouded sacred image but

a book, scroll, black words

on white copied in love & awe

because truth's beyond

distinction, to name's to

dissolve in fire & air.

the past, the past, as told

as lived, you can't argue

with that, its meaning's

that it was, you are

.

Hojo-san: "East, West

a person of zazen is the

same. grandmother mind

the kind heart, is imagination,

feeling for another

see them as yourself

takes imagination, imagination

expands the heart. one day

woke heard sound

in both ears — sudden

hearing loss. my eyes don't

work right either. age is

slowly melting my body. with

each loss there's gain:

my ears, my eyes, more mine

now than ever, before not.

so when I lose my life to death

will my life be owned by me

more then than it ever was?"

Hakusan's sacred rushing water

stories told again and again

sound of water flows by Rinso-In,

Eiheiji, the same quiet sound

brings eternal peace, water's

not the same

many waters flow down

in channel : good place

for a temple here

.

sleeping in tea room

open up doors & windows

air out the mold

such elegant surroundings

for inelegant people

each door, each wall, re-

member where you are or

bump head, as I do

.

JULY 18.10. YAIZU. RINSO-IN

Eiheiji zuisse, bowing to

Dogen: purify robes with

Incense; arrive, rehearse.

Bathe, eat, sleep but

Koe-san seems not to sleep

Arrives late, rises early

Sleeps on back, unmoving

Summer heat ; killing

Robes soaked through, asah

Zagu needs sewing's

Hard to grip & slides

Off arm, hossu flips,

Tassel's dangling, just as

Instructed – long, long

Eiheiji corridors, many steps,

Sizes, steep & steeper

Stopping, bowing, going on in

Little red slippers paying

Respects to past, "Mr

Generation" today's

Tendo Nyojo's day, sun comes

Out after night of thunder & rain

Early morning Jodo Hall as monks sit

All this written before

And again & again

They were life, I am here

You will be there, here

Time's specific & eternal

Not external – no outside

In time – no outside at

All, ashes, ashes, all fall

Down, rise up side-stepping

Three steps, bow to Guest

Director, no mistakes, just

As if nothing happened

Flowing movement in Hatto

Under golden parasols

Golden lotus offerings

Murmured chanting, heart throb

Drum – bow and leave

Shingyo, Dharani, incense –

Many bows, hossu flips

Koe and I in perfect time

Together, short & tall

Big & small, old & young

Together : photo! photo!

Red koromo & white okesa

It's Hojo-san! Abbot's

Representative! Congratu-

Lations, Congratulations, bow

& receive. Temple Ad-

Ministrator: "Zazen is for

Happiness for all people every-

Where, none left out, con-

Gratulations on becoming

A priest!" Sweets & tea

Plum & sweet water

It all makes sense once you

See the logic, logic gone

Wild in detail & respect

Young monks shout & clean,

Race down hallways, bow

And breathe in a blur

.

Japanese snack area on

Highway, cacophony of vending

Machines deep fried

Junkfood, paper cups of hot

Green tea free with any

Purchase, garish lights &

Crowds, bikers, children,

Cool Air Machines blast

In parking lot where earnest

Cops direct traffic with their wands

.

at   the   top

of   this   mountain

there's   a   spirit

protects   this   place

.

cleaning sect of Kosho's

dad long ago. buckets, rags

knock on doors & say,

"please sir, may I clean

your toilet?" and he says

"oh thank you but you see

I've just cleaned it"

but maybe not – old person,

busy person, you enter & clean

go on to next

so in bakery those long years ago

Kosho made us clean & clean

again, with a dogged joyful

spirit. one member of the sect

elected to the Diet, cleaned

the toilets there, Japan so

pure, so kind, nothing for one's

self, no fame, no fortune, no

purple robe, live in the

mountains, clean the toilet,

sit quiet, listen to the water

.

JULY 19. 10. YAIZU. RINSO-IN

Everywhere you look : something

                    Someone

Never   Nothing

          Always

.

Koe and Michiko his mom

bringing eel cookies, famous

eel cookies, sit, drink tea

compare rakesus. family

connections – my father's

teacher was your grand-

father teacher's sister's

husband!　　　imagine!

.

shoes off, shoes on: where's

　　　shoes

　　　　?

.

last night's zazen sudden

flash of inner light in full

robes, humid heat, all

　　　pores blaze sweat

and fire's in the organs then

evaporation's cooling effect

.

time drum & bell :

　boom　boom　boom　boom

　boom　boom　boom　boom

　dong　dong　dong

old serene sound of ancient

      mountain

.

ants up & down the tree

the children always want to kill them

a fun thing to do, move small

thumb & all ants' fun

spoiled, you can do it!

you are big! Hojo-grandpa

says no don't do that laughs

as they do it all the more

ants that speak in smells

that make chemical trails

that make intricate houses

whose queens lay eggs 20 years

highly intelligent, efficient, lovely

ants, busy ants, somehow gone,

but others now resume their

business, children go on

to other joys —

.

                    but if not then

                    what , enough

imagination ? Genji's

obsession with the little

              purple princess – Genji's

restless heart , beauty ,

intellectual appetites &

              privilege

              high – born

  we fall before you

    fulfilling your every wish

because this is who you

are   -   we   are

each   thing   has

              its   place

in the brocade pattern

              .

Shungo dignified young

    Priest, Kumi

    his lovely wife

    youth , age ,

there's a life to maintain

what can you call this ?

how do you know it ?

duty, honor's bounty

    .

you can argue with

        that but we do not

        argue : it is

how we've always lived

on this mountain

    .

Life's ordered

        In its place

Water flows

        Down the mountain

Temple's here

        At mountain's top

The valley

        And its people

Protected

    .

many sorts of crickets

very loud at night, some

like sticks rubbing, others

like children crying, water

sounds all the time bird

sounds morning & evening

.

boom   boom   boom

boom   boom   boom

dong dong dong

                ping! ping! ping!

.

Twenty chairs in

Kaisando for mem-

Orial service today

Family all in

Black, kids too

Shungo chants, offers

Flowers, incense, candles

Long time there

Beyond steep stairs

In small room

Where statues preside

Over solemn feeling

We do this

For gone ones

Our forefathers we

Loved & love

Our duty now

Others later on

Makes life firm

.

bench : another

photo : bye-bye

where to find ten

good hossu & not

have to pay so

much China's got cheap

ones, good ones too

but how gain access

to China, find one

who sells such things

Matsumotoya will sell

at very high price

yak hair, yes

& 21 centimeter handles

maybe make a deal

for spiritual power no

doubt is gained when

you have got the

right & proper stuff

.

JULY 20. 10. YAIZU. RINSO-IN

living in tearoom's not

easy everything's too low

you must never hurry

lest you caroom through

paper door or delicate

bamboo window you must

bend over always slightly

walking room to tiny

room for unexpectedly a

ceiling element appears lower

than the rest you

crack head maybe several

times a day &

if tall even entering

leaving a room must

constant pay close attention

can't close door without

standing just so facing

door full so can't

anticipate next door must

completely concentrate on this

door else it stick

maybe you will break

it if just slightly

too rough – not yet

dear Mitsu Suzuki

okasan visited — 97 —

beeline for Hondo

not greeting anyone

bowing, praying, sitting

silent then "welcome

home!" though I

doubt she remembered

us after 17

years she's here

saying hello

Rinso-In all welcome

home place, in photo book

we look at

picture of Suzuki-

roshi leaving Rinso-In

Hoichi with silly

grin behind him

both enjoy some

foolish family joke

no doubt 51

years ago she

self-contained &

dignified still holds

tiny trim body

in elegant grace

hands gesture while

speaking controlled in

self-possessed expressive dance

recites wavering haiku

tells of her

life the school

next door for

children who can't

go to school

every day "hello!"

bringing something to

her, the businessman's

house on the

other side, they

come to stay

one night – "hello!"

"each day I

walk one hour

my job to

know who lives

alone I knock

on their door

& say 'come

out, it is

spring' " & sings

for us a

spring song &

leaves walking resolutely

with her cane

crisp white hippari

with matching pants

fresh & clean

she sings a

good-bye song

.

try not to smell like

        butter

this I can

           say to you

because I am

           your laundress:

and my mother said it to me

.

uh oh, I peed last

    night

        on

           tea

              house

    windowsill

.

10 hossu ; 10 per cent

    discount

    from

  Matsumotoya

    but

  still very expensive

.

it can't but

in illumined grass

    land

    find

a way to live

    the oneness of things

    the difference of things

  life's flow : with

a single look all's for-

given in a world of constant

life&death, kindness

      without limit   :

        violets

        in   snow

.

small drum-chime

vajra bell, silver :

song

        singing when one's gone

        when you can't

        think about them

        because of all

        the arrangements

singing the song   ,   time for

        tears

.

walls around temple, walls,

gates,

walls,walls,walls

fence .   door .

        window   .

        entryway .

steep steps up

        &

"I'm being stared at"

.

Having nothing to say

I do   ,   I don't say

saying   ,   doing –

        >maintenance<

    maintain the past,

    the future

    maintain the nation

    the ethos

    maintain the buildings

    the land

so   nothing

    to

    say

.

someone coming to see me

comes to see himself

comes to see his representative

    trunks of the trees

    are bare below

    being limbed

    for future timber

he says "I wanted to meet

    you   now

    here I am"

    precise, elegant

    hand gestures

    in every thing we do

    creating the possibility

    of jokes in the way

    you open something

    pick something up

.

there's no space

no land

no seeing, you don't see anything

so no feeling – no social

the others are space, they're

       time

space/time/land   (grass

           land go in

             illumined)

is as they are – they are

    as you – you are

there, in them, they're

as if – (it's so)

      in you

so it's lonely

      &

there's no being

            alone

"only a concept"

beyond concept so you do –

life's   action   acting

life's maintenance . cleaning

    &

    cleaning again . that's

     time/space

you

&

me

"going beyond concepts,

thoughts, ideas"

is a concept, thought, idea

but you can't do it!

(without violating concepts,

thoughts, ideas

how can you *be*

without concepts, thoughts, ideas

the idea of a chair

the idea of a person

fixed, concrete idea

wall,wall,wall,gate,

fence,window – stone

stream

cloud ,,,,,,,,,,,,,,,,,,,,

.

JULY 21.10. YAIZU. RINSO-IN

when you are dead things

improve, people feed

you, bow to

you, bring many

treats, respect, their

daily activity maintains

your memory and

you don't have

to sweat in

summer freeze in

winter eat or

poop, talk, get

your feelings hurt

get mad, disgusted

feel tired, sick

you don't have

to die

in this world

we take care

of, honor our

dead, the whole

of our activity

dedicated to them

our life keeps

the past alive

.

in this world

(another world) we

figure out new

things to do

we figure the

past is dead

and gone what

use could it

possibly have now

unless it tells

us a better

way to live

or is maybe

material for a

theme park or

interesting tourist spot

the past was

fine but we

have to live

our lives now

we have problems

.

crickets say

      seeseeseeseeseeseeseeseeseeseeseeseesee

then say

      heeheeheeheeheeheeheeheeheeheeheeheehee

.

all the onerous things

that must be done

outsourced to foreign others

who do their work

at night when the

real people are out

entertaining or being entertained

.

everyone

works

        don't you know

    what   real

    work   is

      ?

quiet temple day,

cleaning tea house

wiping many kinds

of wood, silk

duster for bamboo

rafters damp rag

for tatami and

rough broom for

roof and walkways

.

time to talk

drink tea what

do we think

about it all

what can we

remember and reflect

how do we

feel our lives

.

It's go in

                        horizontal

it's be home

"welcome

home" here in

Rising Sun's Land

of delicate people

vertical

each one has his place

walls, walls,

no task-frustration here

barrier

patiently viewed open arms

in one

so look up, look back and

there's

comfort in your place

tint

of time dyes one's skein of

years

wholly home yet each one lonely

horizontal

people's inner walking

horizontal

inner's outer also

vertical

all hold up sky, each

it's go

in momentary sphere-ing

      lost

each one's thought a mirror

      back ....

.

JULY 24. 10. TOKYO

Leaving Rinso-In:

      many bows

      to one

           and all

many cars

      to train station

"Better to be

      completely ignorant

knowing a little

      's worse

than knowing nothing at all"

.

Shungo-san & Chitose

behind cyclone fence

waving   ,   faux

                    weeping

            faux fence rattling

            feigning to escape

            their beautiful

                                temple

                        life

.

Shinkansen to Yoko-

                    hama

                    to

                    Sojiji

"monastery that

holds everything"

                    huge

            guardian kings

        furious as sumo wrestlers

            but not as fat

industrial architecture

concrete pillars

"largest hatto in the

                    world"

and two kilometers of

polished wood floor plat-

            forms

wiped each day by over-

       wrought monks

.

and here's Koe-san

to meet us in Shizuoka

white towel on head in heat

wheeling suitcase from station

down busy city street

up steep sidewalk

through Sojiji's massive gate

"I will write for you

I will speak in English

You will please pay

For ceremony and for your

       group"

waiting in gift shop

buying incense

.

... and Ryuki-san too

       now

     there are three

       of us

wearing red rakesus

puzzling in two languages

over complicated

ceremony instruction book

.

"segoy: great   ,

wonderful   ,   the

Top!!"

.

Tettsu says, "Now time

to take bath, you

two"

but not Koe-san : he

thinks

Koe-san is

a woman

"... I am not woman

I am man!"

Ryuki-san & Koe-san

have a great laugh

over this

"He is so beautiful

I think he woman"

Tettsu explains   ,   no

one is

embarrassed

.

Bhadabhadra,

bodhisattva of the bath   :

bow & bathe

"Not bass, a fish

not bat, to hit a ball,

bath - with tongue

between teeth"

    hard to say

cockroach upside down

walks on ceiling

    4

   of them

  lurking around

   Rinso-In

 fast & big

"cockroach in my

    suitcase!"

3:30 – wake up.

"Please put on color-

   ful

  robe belt"

But I haven't got

  colorful robe belt

"I will get for you"

    yellow, not

   "mouse color"

as I ordered from Matsu-

motoya

"Do you know mouse

not *mouth* with

tongue between teeth

???????"

"Yes I know mouse I

like mouse   :

Tom   &   Jerry!"

.

zazen — bow to

kentan man

turn around

sit more —

.

— pop up — back to room to

change into

okesa & bessu

okesa Sojiji

style

tied but not

flipped back & tucked

so that it constant

flaps out one must

constant re-tuck, no

that's Eiheiji style, in

Sojiji style you don't flap

& tuck so panels

flop, ties showing so

easier! Sampai's different

too : you stand on zagu,

bow, stand off, prostrate

must remember these small

details as you bow & walk

even run down long

polished (& slippery!)

corridors in shiny red slippers

that at least

       almost

           this time

                           fit

Keizan altar high above

In biggest Hatto in the world

Kneeling, wash hands

To purify then sidestep up

Sampai! Daiten!

But tenzagu for bows to

Right, left, & center again

After shoko

In choki

In dim

Early-morning

Pre-dawn pre-light

Then sidestep down

Other side bow to Memorial

Hall Master

March round tatami

Following Koe-san who

Follows Ryuki-san who

Follows the leader

.

Sojiji style : red nyoi,

Not whisk

Red okesa

Very fast shoko

In unison

Three kobaku

Certificate from Abbot

In mitred hat

Bow when you hear your

                        name

Come up when you hear it

                              again

Chant sutra   :   know

When to bow   :   know

When to lift your head

"Do you know when?

That is most important

thing, the only important"

"No, I do not know"

        Here is what

        You must say

        In Japanese

In a very loud

Voice

As you bow to Ryoban:

GOzuiki, arigato goZAImasu"

        Very   loud

eat   plum

drink   tea

drink   more tea

but place certificate

on top of the cake

you do not eat

.

Failed to see

      that a person

      in the past

      is what they *are*

      doing, are

and aren't that

then & now

      (both)

      so

everyone's interpreted

everyone's got

tongue between teeth

saying I am this or that

here or there

now or then – later

I want this & that

so what's a person

that there isn't as

      much

      fear

here

is according to how the

organs function

in making something

of the data

for one's self — it isn't

              like that

             isn't as

        one has been taught

           AT   ALL

.

training young men

to stand & walk

to speak

to be spoken to

respecting the past

.

drives away without a

        glance, invisible

.

Rinso-In screens:

      red trees

      cris-crossed bamboo

      straight   new

      shoots   tapered

        at tip

      big ocean waves

      bird on rock – red

      (green sea , white

            waves)

another rock washed

with white waves

just   as

      where we

      live''''''''''''''''''''''''''''''''''''''

.

lonely   bird

lonely   rock

.

Sojiji : tea

with Kansho monk

in room   with

          chairs!

          sofas!

and picture of sumo

          man honoring

          Sojiji with

          his massive

          presence   (yet

now   there's

sumo   scandal

match   been

cancelled :   disgrace!)

"you have practiced

zazen 40 years. these

twelve monks are your

disciples. you will

return to California"

lamplight, words

      here

      now

   in   Tokyo

   old   Edo

power   problem?

move   capitol

then   write

  of it   now

.

Koe-san wants to hang out

with us, he wants to practice

English, we are unusual, we

are interesting. "kind eyes."

we appreciate him! we

love him! he is so cute,

so sweet. "my language

is body language, OK but

some deeper thing can't

say." waves hands indica-

ting, no, not, crosses

wrists: "no!" "*dame*!"

he says, we think "dammit"

cute English – "I pay

own lunch!" No, *dame*,

not good you pay. at

train station Koe-san

changes from neat priest

traveling costume to cut-

off jeans, funny tee

shirt, black watch

cap though it is

100° "so no one see I

am priest." Koe-san

ordained in elementary

school, always he wanted

to be priest, like his dad

playing bass (not "bath")

in temple, people gathering

happy: "like that, peace-

ful place." Koe plays

contemporary jazz trumpet,

his sister steel drum: 3

CD's. please come to

America. I will come. I

will study English hard.

Ganbatte! loud waitress

noodle shop owner, room

full of us raising glass

of beer: "Omedetou!"

Finish!

Very hot in Tokyo

Broad cross-walk

Everyone crosses

Many hundreds

Wait then walk

.

writing down

what happens

is that so?

.

People all around

I'm in

Another world

"Writing as an Aid

To Memory"

Writing as a memorial

To the past

Writing as

Withdrawal from the present

Writing as the present

A question

        of

        words....................................

  .

confounded

confabulation

  .

Tokyo zoo, the

        elephants

gathering their grass

in flexible trunks

swirl & hurl

        into open mouth

        & chew

        as ears flap

sun bears, pigeon-toed

& big-toed, claws, un-

        gainly

back & forth

wait by door

for food in heat

Sumatrian tiger

paces, pisses up

under tree branch

thick leg of meat

chained in place

in market many

used kimono, we

bought nuts – extra

nuts, here are more

peanuts, Nike, Crocs,

Ralph Lauren

.

so many fish, all sizes

dried bonito looks like

piece of wood (shave

for flakes for miso soup)

octopus tentacle

dried squid, all kinds

seaweed, mushroom

.

hot in Tokyo

maybe is a record

not

     "Scenes of life in the

          Capitol"

not

     "Old Japan"

not

     Genji's delicate

     hand, his delicate

     words, making elegant

     satisfaction of desire

without guilt or

concern for others,

class is all, beauty's

all if beautiful

anything can be

done, everything's good

gentle world

except for peasants

starving in

winter-time

but all must

suffer & die

in the world of dew

says Genji

wiping away

a tear

"Scenes of Life in the Capitol"

.

KIYOTAKA ASAHARA

"The World of Emotions"

exploding   head

revealing   sheets of content

above calm   horizon line

many shoes   ,   some

darkly smudged   ,   oozing

feelings from down here

at the feet

a few birds   ,   distant

motorcyclist

.

2 kilometers of dark wood

floor   flows

    I

    don't

    flow

    in ....

[thought in dream

  with good quality

  brightly colored

  (orange, yellow)

  Japanese underwear]

    don't

    flow in

.

    train,train

  wall,wall,wall

.

"modern" is "western"

to be modern

       is   to   be

   not   what   we   are

to be

      other than that

  free to do as we please

  but what pleases

to follow our ways

ways of the ancients, the

      fathers

willful _____ stupendous

"............ yet the retreating figure

      of the Master

      somehow brought

      tears to my eyes

      I was profoundly

      moved, for reasons

      I myself do not

      understand

      In that figure

      walking absently

      from the game

      there was the still

      sadness

      of another world"

Huge metal Torii gate,

      War Memorial

      Temple – war

and   gods

our   nation

    die

        for the people

        letters   home

       "please   pray

             for me

    I am glad to die

      for you"

train,plane,boat

      honor

kids wearing red war

uniforms, carrying

gun replicas

drinking tea next to us

in War Memorial

coffee shop

.

so many words English

words

    everyone speaks

    English, says

    "I do not speak

        English"

.

where there's care and

consideration of others

where there's no self

without reference to others

there's face

for others — so not

    much

    truth

we say what ought to

    be

    the case

we do not say

     what is

          the case

          our face

          must not

reveal the unacceptable

we   say   what   isn't   so

as   true   if   it   should

          be   so

          for   you

.

shouting noodle lady

louder than we are

"do you chant

Shingyo?"

brings you what you want

whether you want it

          or not

.

ando – you sleep in

        little tatami box

        raised above floor

        under which you store

            your shoes

        lit brightly

        shower's just barely

        large enough to stand in

        how   put on

           clothes

             ?

mesh screens over

all windows and on

            up

four flights to

   roof so

windows softly glow

seen from outside /

        polished

        green

        façade

in   &   out

day   &   night

  tiny Tokyo spaces

antique market near

war memorial

statues, tea things

I do not like to see

in museums but like

          to see

          here

(I can feel them

     can imagine their

     use)

.

famous Tokyo fish market

          5 AM

fat white frozen tuna

auctioneers on small platforms

shout & point

bidders digitate

five minutes & done

out to vast covered

               market

where we're not supposed

               to go

     avoiding

          the whirling forklifts

everywhere

everything

imaginable

from the sea

(even including gooey-ducks)

bustling through narrow aisles

taking pictures

Japanese fish industry guys

equivalent to cowboys

do not have the grace

of Kyoto teamen

rough, smoking, yelling,

products of their trade

disgorged somehow

out onto street

we eat sashimi break-

fast, find

train

buy ticket home

on dark ocean

in lightning

where there's no

        horizon >>>>>>>>>

later setting sun & rising moon

.

moat

        for doomed

                castle

lasted 19 years

though biggest & brightest ever seen

never rebuilt but moat's

tall thick walls

of fitted rectangular stones

& brown churning water chasm

remain – joggers

circle the parameter _____

    grassy expanse

    through forest

    with dwarf bamboo

    undergrowth

.

Japanese : vague

English   : unforgiving

.

    Keigo, how to talk

In context of who,

what, you are when

she, she, he, it is

near _ now

.

miroku   .   okami

.

days and months

are the travelers of eternity

so are the years

that pass by

...

A Zen Buddhist priest, abbot, and teacher, and author of many collections of poetry, Norman Fischer received his MFA from the University of Iowa Writers' Workshop. He has been active in the San Francisco Bay Area writing community since the 1970's, loosely associated with the Language Movement. His latest prose work is *Training in Compassion*. Forthcoming from University of Alabama Press is his *Experience: Essays on Thinking, Writing, Language and Religion*.

TIN⊦ISH

Also available from TinFish Press:

Donovan Kūhiō Colleps, *Proposed Additons*. 2014, $14

Lehua M. Taitano, *A Bell Made of Stones*. 2013, $18

Steve Shrader, *The Arc of the Day | The Imperfectionist*. 2013, $24

J. Vera Lee, *Diary of Use*. 2013, $16

Jack London is Dead: Contemporary Euro-American Poetry in Hawai'i (and Some Stories), edited by Susan M. Schultz. 2012, $20

Ya-Wen Ho, *last edited [insert time here]*. 2012, $13

Maged Zaher, *The Revolution Happened and You Didn't Call Me*. 2012, $15

Jai Arun Ravine, แล้ว *and then entwine*. 2011, $18.

Elizabeth Soto, *Eulogies*. 2010, $14.

Kaia Sand, *Remember to Wave*. 2010, $16

Daniel Tiffany, *The Dandelion Clock*. 2010, $15

Paul Naylor, *Jammed Transmission*. 2009, $16

Lee A. Tonouchi, *Living Pidgin: Contemplations on Pidgin Culture*, 2nd edition. 2009, $14

Lisa Linn Kanae, *Sista Tongue*, 2nd edition. 2008, $10

Meg Withers, *A Communion of Saints*. 2008, $14

Craig Santos Perez, *from unincorporated territory [hacha]*. 2008, $15

Hazel Smith, *The Erotics of Geography*. 2007, $18

Barbara Jane Reyes, *Poeta en San Francisco*. 2006, $13

For other TinFish Press publications, including chapbooks and TinFish journals 1-20, visit our website: tinfishpress.com